What are *TRAIN2WIN* Publications?

TRAIN2WIN Publications are a series of easy to use training guides which are designed to help define the subject content in a manner that allows the reader to fully understand the information in a way that will help establish the basis for a functional training initiative or program. While not intended to be a complete analysis or study of the identified subject in themselves, each book in the *TRAIN2WIN* Publication series does provide a detailed overview.

TRAIN2WIN Publications take the philosophies outlined in the **TRAIN2WIN Manifesto** (available for purchase on Amazon.com) and applies them in more detail to the respective subject matter of each in the series. The *TRAIN2WIN* Publication series covers the full spectrum of corporate training subjects and issues; ranging from getting new employees hired, sales and customer service training, to harassment and change management.

Each book in the **TRAIN2WIN** Publication series may be used as a presentation / instructor guide, or can also be used as a handbook style tool for those taking a training course. Each Publication addresses its own unique and specific training subject, and all are written in easy to read and understand language.

Each book in the **TRAIN2WIN** Publications Series is also supported by a companion Power Point Presentation that can be ordered for a small additional fee ($9.95) by contacting us directly at **TRAIN2WIN** by telephone (303-947-8989), by email (TMindala@gmail.com), or by simply contacting us on our website (Train2win.weebly.com) to send us a request.

COACH
TO
WIN

A coach is defined in Webster's dictionary as follows:

"One who coaches; as a private tutor who assists students in their studies. An instructor in athletics. To prepare for public examination or contest by private instruction; to train. To instruct as, or receive instruction from a coach."

I personally define a mentoring coach as one who possesses the knowledge and skills necessary to mentor and instruct another how to do a thing better and best achieve the agreed upon results desired. In many cases it requires the ability to teach individuals to become part of an organizational team. In the specific case of the athletic coach I would add that these coaches in particular endeavor to make those they work with better than they think they can be.

We should add here that a mentoring coach in comparison to the training instructor typically works alongside the employees he or she is assigned to coach in an associated or managerial supervisory role. There are times as well when a coach in a specific situation is simply a more experienced employee on the team who has been given the responsibility to teach other employees basic skills.

We also should note at this time that for the purposes of our discussion a manager / supervisor is defined as an employee who has been assigned the task to manage or supervise others in the organization.

This **Coach to Win Publication** is all about the importance of coaching in the corporate training environment, how to coach the members of a team in a way that promotes improvement, and how to take better advantage of what the coaching process can offer.

While we discuss many of the aspects and issues regarding what's involved in how we train employees in the corporate environment, nothing in my opinion is any more important than how we consider the ways we coach and mentor those we work directly with and supervise. And, here's why.

The vast majority of training initiatives and methods we in business undertake happen away from the on-site job circumstance with no direct involvement to make the connection for the most part, while mentored coaching conversely by it's very nature must be done directly on the job to be successful. Sure, there are at times a "classroom" instructional aspect to the coaching process, but in comparison to other teaching / instructional methods it always takes a back seat to hands on job instruction when we mentor and coach.

But, even though most corporate managers and supervisors would readily agree if asked that coaching is one of their key responsibilities, precious little real or organized thought typically goes into the process. Most mentored coaching, if done at all in any sort of organized fashion, tends to be haphazard at best and absolutely dysfunctional at worst with little or no planning for the most part. This is unfortunate.

And, I have to be honest and admit that it was quite late in my own managerial career before I truly recognized the importance and benefits of doing one on one and group coaching in an organized consistent manner to improve the performance of those I supervised.

How valuable do I think coaching is?

Let me put it this way, if I was running a company with a limited training budget I would make mentored coaching my highest priority and favor it over the more expensive training options available. Why...?

- Coaching is far less expensive to implement and manage than comparable training initiatives.

- Coaching can rely upon in house subject experts who are intimately knowledgeable about your processes and will have greater credibility than outside consultants.

- Coaching can be focused on specific knowledge, tasks, and / or methods that give it more immediate impact.

- The vast majority of coaching can take place right on the job where the coach can see the impactive results of the instruction.

- Coaching takes little or no time out of job applications, and can in the majority of cases become part of the job routine itself.

- Coaching can be done on a consistent basis as the need is recognized.

- Coaching lends itself easily to change as various circumstances and priorities change, and can be adjusted accordingly with little effort.

- Coaching can be customized easily to the needs of individuals and groups.

Let me stress before we go forward that I'm NOT saying that coaching should supplant instructional training or that they are mutually exclusive. The very best

of training programs will in fact include both instructional training and on the job mentored coaching as part of the initial and ongoing training regimen.

That said, I still say that in an environment where funds are limited on the job mentored coaching comparatively tends to be a far more cost effective and more impactful use of resources in general. In my opinion, which is based on more than 3 decades of experience, you literally get "more bang for your buck" through coaching than any other single training technique if it's organized to be well aligned to goals and objectives, is consistent, and is directly focused on all of the most up to date needs of the organization.

CONTENTS

"Coaching is one of the most important duties
all managers, supervisors, and mentors
have in the corporate business world;
so why is it that we pay it so little attention?"

Thom Mindala

By it's very nature the mentored coaching process involves a direct one on one and face to face interaction between the instructor (who is usually a managing supervisor) and the student employee in the vast majority of cases. There are instances where, just like the athletic team, a managerial coach can and will use his or her talents to mentor an entire group of employees or associates.

Training is many times described as the nuts and bolts that hold things together to build an effective team within an organization. If we allow ourselves to assume that this is true, then mentored coaching becomes the glue that keeps everything from falling apart and makes the training process cohesive in a manner that improves the performance of both individuals and the group as a whole.

Where training initiatives (even long term programs) tend to be one and done with follow-up processes to be repeated occasionally as determined by the needs of the organization, coaching is the essential skill that actually constitutes the follow-up of many training regimens to be executed on a continuous basis in order to drive home the learned knowledge and skills to the targeted audience. Coaching is what must go on between training exercises and after if what we train is to be both successful and sustainable over time.

The real difference between classic training techniques and those used by the mentoring coach is that training typically identifies any number of related subjects to address and learn while coaching sessions usually address only one.

Here's the problem:

As important as ongoing coaching is to an organization's ultimate success it's typically either taken for granted or even entirely ignored as an organized training technique. And, this is truly unfortunate because coaching not only will become one of the most sustainable parts of any training regimen if correctly focused upon, but by it's very nature will be the most cost effective to the organization.

While organizations are quick to spend millions of hard earned corporate dollars on any number of "glitzy" training initiatives they often ignore the far less expensive less spectacular needs that come with the need to coach what is taught afterwards.

What do I mean? I call it the Myth of the Tickle Down Effect.

The company pulls all of it's manager supervisors into long and expensive training sessions where they not only expect but implore the participants to take all that they've just learned and share it with the rest of their teams. A good idea in principle, but if you don't concentrate on how what you ask is to actually be done then your results will necessarily be either limited or nonexistent.

This is where effective mentored coaching skills come in, and they don't just happen because you have what you think is an experienced group of manager supervisors to rely upon. You have to make them happen.

Our objective with this Coach to Win discussion is to help you understand the need to coach, realize that there are some basic skills involved, and know that there is a process that must be followed to make sure that everything stays aligned to identified corporate goals and objectives and remains relevant to those being trained. Some of the subjects we will discuss are:

- Hiring the type of prospective team members in the beginning who will commit themselves to the coaching process as supervisory managers.

- Identifying and then empowering manager supervisors with the skills they need to become effective coaches to their team.

- Using mentored coaching techniques to drive home employee training.

- Using the same mentored coaching techniques to build productive teams.

- Using mentored coaching to keep the corporate talent pool full.

Here's the bottom line, having in place an organized and well aligned mentored coaching process throughout your organization is one of the most functional and cost effective training tools in your organizational development toolbox.

- Mentored coaching is easy to design and implement.

- You already have in place an experienced pool of instructors to draw on.

- It requires no special facilities or equipment.

- It doesn't have to cost valuable dollars and resources to be effective.

In many companies a stronger reliance on mentored coaching techniques that are well aligned to the needs and objectives of both the organization and the individual employee will actually save money over time in the training budget. Why?

- You don't have to go out and hire that expensive consultant to train your people.

- Mentored coaching by it's very nature doesn't require an employee to spend unproductive time away from the job.

- Mentored coaching most often allows you to get feedback on results far quicker than the typical training regimen.

Here you are, totally overwhelmed by an enormous pile of responsibilities the company has heaped on your managerial plate, and now you're being asked to also be a coach to the hapless souls who work for you on top of it.

You're probably asking... "What's in it for me? There's already not enough time in the day to do what I have to do to get my own job done, so where am I ever going to find the time to make it easier for those guys?"

"And besides, after I spend all of the time it will take to use my vast knowledge and experience to coach them up the company is going to take them away from me anyway, which means I will just have to start all over with another bunch of poor souls who are going to make my managerial life a living nightmare."

And believe me when I say that we've all been there!

Well, here's the actual truth of the matter...

- Yes, it will frankly take a small additional bit of your already tight and overworked managerial schedule to focus on being an effective coach to those who work for you.

- I will point out, however, that the smartest of the coaches learn quickly that they don't have to do all of the coaching themselves. They realize that they have at their fingertips associated others who are more than willing to help.

- But, here's the secret that only those who have made the leap and committed themselves to becoming an organized and effective coach know... that if and when they do spend the time to coach on a consistent basis it will ultimately make their lives so much easier.

Why is this you ask?

- Organized and focused coaching by a supervisory mentor always improves the performance of both individuals and groups of employees.

- Time consuming issues and problems go down as a result.

- Conversely, attitudes and morale go up at the same time.

- And, before you know it, things are getting done without you having to ask or harp.

- So at the end of the day, instead of taking more precious time out of an already hectic schedule, the mentored coaching you do actually ends up saving you time.

Managers and supervisors who have committed themselves to being a mentoring coach to those they lead understand that by building up individuals they are building the strength of the entire team. And, when they build the strength of the whole team, two things happen...

- Performance and productivity improves dramatically.

- The manager supervisor's job gets easier which then allows more time to do the things that are truly important to the department or business.

Coaching Saves Time
and
Great Teams
Have
Great Coaches

Believe it or not, effective coaching doesn't just happen...

It would be wrong to assume that coaching and mentoring don't take place without planning beforehand. Mentoring of a sort does in fact always take place wherever humans congregate and coaching among team members is a naturally occurring activity that does in fact take place when you have experienced individuals working in tandem with those not as experienced. But, here's the key... is the mentoring and coaching that goes on going to be properly aligned with the needs of the organization or will it be effective, and can you assume that it will remain truly relevant to those being coached?

No truly aligned and effective coaching program can exist without the commitment of both those who are responsible to coach those they work with and those who stand to benefit from being coached by their more experienced associates.

"I call it to coach and be coached"

No, truly effective and functional coaching doesn't just happen all by itself. To be functional and effective, mentored coaching takes both an effort on the part of the one's tasked with doing the instructional coaching and those who have been targeted for what needs to be learned.

- Coaches need to learn the basic skills they require to mentor those they are tasked to train in a positive and consistent manner that's well aligned to all of the ideas and processes involved.

- Student employees have to have an attitude that allows them to be open to the coaching they need to become better at what they do.

A commitment to coach and be coached also doesn't just happen...

Coaches aren't born, but are created by hard work and learned skills. Just the same, an employee who demonstrates the ability to manage and supervise isn't by definition a coach.

- Coaching skills should be included in any new managerial or supervisory "leadership" training.

- If a strong "coaching culture" is what you desire in your organization you have to encourage it by both requiring a commitment on the part of all prospective manager supervisors, and by providing the necessary skills to make coaching techniques both relevant and effective.

- One of the best ways to establish and encourage a strong mentored coaching culture within an organization is to establish a set of rewards to those who do so most effectively.

Many companies make the mistake of just assuming that the new employees they hire will be willing to be mentored and coached to improve themselves. We've all seen it when a newly hired employee who appears at first to have great potential, turns out to be a "diva" of sorts who thinks he or she knows it all after a few short months, and isn't willing to listen to any suggestions.

- Frankly, if you want to insure a commitment from newly hired employees, your expectations as such should be included in the job search and interviewing processes.

In partnership with the operational obligations of the manager supervisor, there is no more important task than to mentor and coach members of the team to become more cohesive and productive. And, anybody who has ever known me will tell you that my personal belief is that the coaching piece is the far more important supervisory role because when it's properly in place and done according to aligned goals and standards, the operational pieces will then all fall into place.

One of the first keys to any successful coaching program is that you must have in place the manager supervisory personnel who possess all of the necessary skills to mentor and coach those who work for them in a "proper manner" that's aligned directly to all of the organization's goals, methods, and objectives.

One of the worst assumptions we make in the corporate world is when we identify a successful employee and promote him or her into a management position without offering the instructional training necessary for the employee to succeed in his or her new supervisory position.

- Previous experience and proven success in the field are both necessary and valuable assets for those tasked with managing others.

- Previous success and experience alone don't, however, guarantee that the employee will become an effective manager supervisor. Frankly, the skill sets to do so are completely different.

- To become both a successful manager and mentoring coach to others on the team, it's the obligation of the organization to provide those identified to do so the required tools and basic skills they need.

The two worst things we must avoid as mentoring coaches are:

- The newly promoted manager supervisor is one of the most successful individuals the company has ever had in the field, so he has been promoted so that others can learn from his experience and skills. Here's the problem:

The newly promoted manager lacks the necessary supervisory skills that will give him the ability to coach the rest of his team, so he's forced to rely only on his own personal experience and methods. This ultimately leads to a "this is how I did it" approach to mentored coaching which over the long term is not at all functional or even credible.

- And then, there's the negative coach who always points out the mistakes made by members of his or her team. Two things happen here. The first is that the targeted employee gets embarrassed in front of his or her peers and, second, he or she, is presented with a negative circumstance that poorly impacts self confidence. Again, not functional or credible.

Both of the above need to be avoided at all costs by the mentoring coach if he or she wishes to be successful over time. There's nothing wrong with relying on past personal successes and / or experiences as references that establish credibility, but to do so as the only coaching strategy is sorely limited at best and will ultimately be poorly received by others. Even more so, the negative coach is doomed to failure as the morale of the team slips and its members simply quit paying attention over time.

- Mentoring coaches must rely on a variety of methods and experiences to share with the team and individuals he or she is coaching.

- Mentoring coaches must always be positive in their approaches, especially in front of others.

The coaches role is obvious... to mentor and coach other less experienced employees the necessary ideas, processes, methods, and skills to get the job done according to the organization's objectives and goals. And this would not only be true in and of itself, but if carried out with no other objective in mind it all alone would be a great and beneficial contribution to the organization. However, mentored coaching offers yet another valuable opportunity not to be ignored or lost, which is that the coaching mentor can learn he or herself from those he or she coaches.

So, the truth is that the organizational or managerial coach actually has two important roles, not just one:

- To coach the required ideas, skills, processes, and methods to those he or she works directly with as determined by the agreed upon goals and objectives of the company.

- To learn from those he or she coaches in a manner that brings a steady stream of new ideas and methods into the organization

The organizational coaches training role

Once again, the coaches role as a training mentor is given and obvious. The goal here is to harness the experience and skills of managers, supervisors, and even other untitled employees with specific skills and experiences they have so they can be shared in a manner that passes that knowledge and skills to others.

The organizational coaches learning role

A coaches learning role isn't as obvious, but is almost as important as his or her training role. To stay relevant and dynamic, every organization must rely on new ideas that come from outside its own cultural experience. And, the best source for those new ideas are the new members of the team brought on board.

"I call it the give and take benefit"
"Others call it new blood"

Most everybody understands how the coaching process delivers the knowledge and skills employees need to become more successful, but few of us understand the opportunity that new employees offer from their own past experiences or unaffected perspective.

- New employees, especially those who have experiences with other organizations in their past, can provide valuable insight and ideas for how things can work differently or better.

- New employees brought into an organization can offer a valuable outside perspective about how you interact and do things.

The Teach and Learn Dynamic

When you establish a "teach and learn dynamic" throughout your organization between managerial supervisors and their employees you will have done much to guarantee that your company will stay "alive and dynamic" in a manner that will keep it up to date and relevant in the corporate marketplace.

Who can be a coach?

The answer is any on the team who have been identified as having the necessary experience and skills to mentor others.

Many companies make a huge mistake by assuming that only supervisory or managing personnel alone can qualify to be a coach. And, when they do so they limit themselves by not understanding the value of what every employee potentially has to offer the mentored coaching process.

- Even the newest team members can mentor and help those newly hired employees with some of the more simple tasks in a department.

- Members of any team have specific skills and experiences that can be recognized and shared with others.

- A team of coaches will always be far stronger than a team that relies on only one coach.

- Sharing the mentored coaching responsibility is one of the best ways to build the cohesiveness and diversity of a team.

You can look at it just like a professional football team who has the head coach who oversees all of the strategies, and a pool of assistants who have specific areas of responsibility in the mentoring process. They all have their roles to play, and together they are successful.

In addition, companies shouldn't ignore the opportunities presented by cross departmental coaching. In cases where the company is structured into departments (such as sales, distribution, HR, marketing, operations, etc.) there will be any number of opportunities where the departmental supervisor can reach out and get coaching support from other departmental teams. Classic examples are sales and customer service, or customer service and distribution, or HR and operations.

I do strongly suggest, however, that when coaching responsibilities are shared with non managerial / supervisory employees or associates in other departments in the organization it be done so very carefully and with close supervision to make sure that what is being taught remains consistent and current to all corporate methods and procedures.

Seems simple doesn't it... It's the employee's job to receive the coaching from his or her mentor coach, and learn the knowledge and skills being taught.

Fair enough... but, while this is the essential truth of the employee's role in the coaching / mentoring process, it frankly doesn't go quite far enough.

- It is the new employee's primary role to be the learning student in the mentored coaching process. But, it's not their only role.

- Every new employee who comes into an organization also represents a valuable opportunity for the organization to learn and improve through the past experiences or unique ideas he or she brings to the table.

- The truly interactive coaching process offers a unique opportunity to harness those experiences and ideas.

- The coaching process also allows an organization and it's managing supervisors to validate processes and procedures with new "unfettered" team members in a manner that helps drive improvement and better productivity.

The Empowered Employee

What do I mean by the Empowered Employee? It's simple, the empowered employee is the one who is willing to learn from his or her more experienced peers, shares new ideas with the group from his or her own past experiences, then eventually becomes a mentoring coach in his or her own right.

Here's the problem that every prospective mentoring coach faces... If care isn't taken to avoid doing so your desire to improve what your employees can do and achieve becomes "mindless harping" if a few essential things aren't kept in mind.

RELEVANT - APPLICABLE - CURRENT

First and most important of all, coaching is only effective when it stays relevant and applicable to the job circumstances of those being coached, and is absolutely current and up to date with circumstances, methods, and procedures.

There are 12 individual points of consideration that I identify as essential to the establishment of a truly organized and functional mentored coaching process. Call it an action plan if you will, but taken all together if you pay attention to and focus on what I refer to as **"THE 12 POINTS OF THE COACHING COMPASS"** you will then have in place what can be described as a comprehensive techniques training regimen for prospective coaches in your organization.

12 Points of the Coaches Compass

(1) Have a plan for WHAT you intend to coach

First of all you have to have a plan for what you intend to coach, and it starts by creating a list of priorities based on the knowledge, skills, methods, and processes that are essential to your operation. They must also be important to the organization. And, when doing so a close eye must be kept on Best Practices on all of the elements that you coach.

(2) Have a plan for HOW you intend to coach

Once you know what you plan to coach, you now have to determine how you plan to do it. It's not enough to simply say you want or intend to do it. You have to make a firm commitment to make it happen, then put it into your operational schedule.

(3) Be consistent

Coaching can only be effective if it's done on a consistent and regular basis. And, this is where the commitment get's important, because coaching will ultimately not work as intended and even disappear in the trash heap of a busy schedule if you don't focus on making it happen as a priority daily, weekly, or whenever fits into your unique circumstances. In addition, the essential elements of the message needs to be consistent every time you coach members of your team.

(4) Must be unique

Coaching, to stay both relevant and successful, must always be closely connected to the employee you are addressing. This is essential, because each one of your employees is unique who requires his or her own set of knowledge or skills to learn. Unlike the classic classroom teaching environment coaching must rely strongly on what's uniquely relevant to each employee you coach. While you may coach the very same subject matter to different members of your team, each will require his or her own level of teaching based on his or her level of experience or skills.

In addition, and just as important, each employee that you coach will require a different and unique approach based on his or her personality. To be effective in your coaching it's essential that you recognize and understand this. Some people simply learn faster, while others take a little more time to digest new information, while still others need to try things out to fully understand. These all will require different approaches and techniques to be used by the mentoring coach.

(5) Keep it focused and short

I call it "hard hitting and impactful." Don't allow yourself to confuse coaching with a full blown training session. I guarantee that if you do you will lose the dynamic power that coaching can provide and you will actually risk losing the attention of those you intend to teach. And here's what you need to remember:

- Coaching should stay simple and sessions should always be focused on a single subject, skill, process, method, or policy.

- Coaching sessions should <u>NEVER</u> be longer than 15 or 20 minutes, and 5 to 10 minutes is better. They need to be short, sweet, and to the point.

- Coaching sessions must always include information that can be measured later through the performance of the employee.

(6) Use the E.D.G.E.

I call it the E.D.G.E., which is a goofy acronym I learned from an associate a while back for how an instructor should present information or material in a way that insures that the person receiving it both gets and understands what you're saying.

- **Explain** = A simple explanation of the subject matter
- **Demonstrate** = A demonstration that further explains what you mean
- **Guide** = Assist in understanding with answers to questions
- **Enable** = An opportunity for participants to show understanding

Using the E.D.G.E. is especially important when coaching new skills, processes, or changed methods to employees.

(7) Must be specific

To remain relevant and dynamic your coaching should always be specific (targeted) and never confusing or ambiguous to the employee. And by specific we also mean that it must be consistent from employee to employee, especially in regards to methods, procedures, and policies to be followed.

(8) Be encouraging but insistent

Coaching should <u>NEVER</u> be allowed to become a negative experience for the employee if at all possible. Even the most dire subjects or negative circumstances can be approached in a positive manner, and it's a proven fact that humans react much better to positive re-enforcement than negative feedback. A coaching session is not the proper place for a "butt chewing"

At the same time, if coaching is to remain viable and relative to the operational improvements you seek, then you must become <u>INSISTENT</u> in what you coach. At times I've been known to describe it as "short, sweet, and required learning." Believe me when I say that it can all remain positive as you insist on what you coach as you work with your team.

(9) Make it fun

Good coaches know how to make it fun for those they coach. And, being coached can become a bit tedious if it's not, so don't be afraid to add a bit of spice and joy to what you teach. Involve partners in the coaching process, remember that you don't know it all. And, as an old sports guy, I say that there's always room for a little competition with the appropriate incentives in the coaching environment.

(10) Be flexible

Yes, you must be committed and you must have a dedicated schedule to rely on if coaching is to become a prioritized part of your routine, but at the same time flexibility in your approach will allow you to take advantage of coaching opportunities as they arrive. Don't allow yourself to be such a slave to a schedule or process that you fail to recognize an opportunity that presents itself. When an employee makes a mistake or goofs it can become an excellent opportunity to coach (positive). Another employee does something well and unexpected which then becomes an opportunity to coach the rest of the team as a whole. Regardless, keep your mind open and flexible so that you can see the coaching opportunities as they appear.

(11) Be hands-on and demonstrative

The best coaching approaches include hands-on and demonstrative techniques that allow the employee to experience firsthand how things are supposed to be done according to Best Practice procedures. These are especially true in situations where the mentoring coach is a recognized expert in the subject matter.

(12) Become accountable

To become a successful coach who has a truly functional and productive coaching process there must be accountability by all in the process.

- The mentoring coach must remain accountable to the coaching process by committing to the schedule and what he or she is tasked to coach.

- At the same time those being coached must make themselves accountable for what they learn and how they apply it to the jobs they do.

- And, as any effective coach always does, the coaching mentor must hold the team accountable for the operational improvements intended in the coaching sessions.

- Lastly, both the coach and those being coached must always be open to feedback so that adjustments can be made as needed.

The effective coach always knows and understands in a moment when a coaching opportunity arrives to be taken advantage of. Embrace these 12 compass point skills, and I assure you that your coaching efforts will be rewarded with better performance and fewer operational issues with your team.

WHY LEADING BY EXAMPLE JUST ISN'T GOOD ENOUGH

We've all seen them, and I was in fact one of those for many years who thought the best way to coach the rest of the team was to simply lead by example. And, it goes without saying that to be a credible and effective coach one does in fact have to walk the talk and lead by example. However, there's also no worse example than the coach who claims to others how it should be done one way, then goes about his or her own business in quite another.

However, the truth of the matter is that leading by example all by itself is simply not enough to guarantee that the rest of the team will do things the way they must be done. I've actually seen situations where the leader of the team who sets such a great example how to do things that the rest of the team simply sits back and watches him do it all.

All truly effective team leaders and coaches know and understand the importance of empowering the rest of the team to do their jobs well in a way that contributes to the ultimate success of the operation.

Don't fall into the trap

So many manager supervisors fall into the trap of taking the easier path by simply doing things themselves rather than working with their team members on a consistent basis to coach them up. I know, I've done it. Here's how it works...

- You know it...

- It will take valuable time that you don't have to teach it...

- So, you just do it yourself to get it done.

This is a never ending merry-go-round that I've seen some pretty good manager supervisors fall into at times. The problem is that the team never improves with this approach, and more important, when the time ultimately comes when the team leader suddenly isn't available the rest of the team lacks the skills or experience they need to get the job done properly without him or her presence.

In comparison, the focused and well organized mentor coach uses his or her own example more as an instructional tool to be used on a consistent basis to teach others the skills and techniques they need to improve their own performance.

- He or she does lead and show by example when the opportunities present themselves.

- He or she the follows his or her example with clear explanations to the rest of the team why things are done the way they are.

- He or she always allows team members the opportunities they need to try the newly learned skills or techniques on their own.

- He or she also stays aware that his or her way of doing things may not be the only or even best way for others to do it.

Bottom line, don't let the idea of "leading by example" allow you to get lazy in your mentored coaching responsibilities.

"Talk the talk = Walk the walk"

Every organization talks "career path" even if only by promising prospective or new employees that they represent a place that has a successful future to offer.

Most organizations brag about the chances for future advancement and promotion to those who work hard and become loyal to the company.

What few organizations actually do is what I refer to as "walk the walk" to make sure that what is promised during the job interview actually becomes the reality when the newly hired employee walks onto the job and starts to work.

Being in the right place at the right time

There's no question that opportunities take place for those who are in position to take advantage of them when they occur. And, this is okay and entirely appropriate in any organization. My point is that if you only rely on recognizing that employee who seems to pop up at the most opportune time as your method for advancement and promotion you are in reality relying on the happen stance of unpredictable circumstances, and there is a better way. Far too often promises are made during the hiring process only to have the employee to fall into a "never never land" of confusion later.

Career Path

The really smart organizations have a career path already in place to show new employees what a potential future can look like. These companies also have a tendency to promote from within as a first choice when filling job openings.

Companies who do so are always on the lookout for who in their own organization might be a good fit for another need within the organization. Conversely, I've seen it when a company hires from outside without doing so, then wonders why so many employees give up and leave.

A career path road map in an organization can be as simple as and look something like the following graphic where a new employee can readily see the future potential opportunities he or she may have in a manner that helps determine his or her future with the company.

Operations

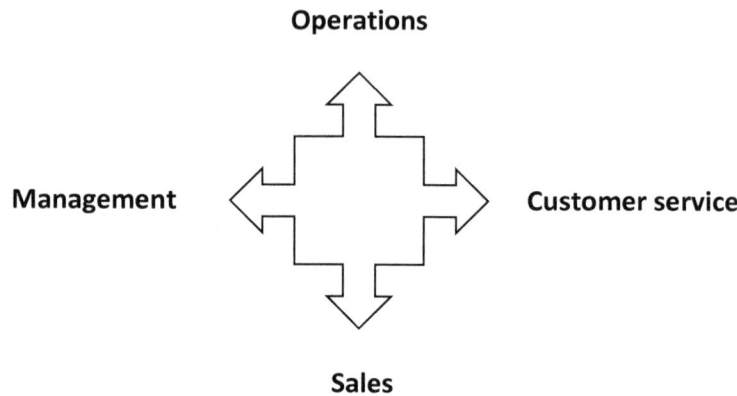

Management   **Customer service**

Sales

Mentored coaching plays a key and essential role in this process, because it's the managing supervisor who must play a direct role in establishing the awareness of a path of future success to new employees.   And here's the interesting and most relevant part, **companies who have in place a mapped out career path and a managerial team committed to it's communication to employees have far fewer issues with morale and a much lower rate of employee turnover than those who don't. And let's face it, morale issues and employee turnover cost money.**

And, the coaches role in the "career path" process is...

- Recruit and hire always with a mind towards potential capabilities that fit organizational needs.

- During the mentored coaching process seek out and identify those same skills for when opportunities for advancement and promotion come about.

- Make sure that management is aware of the individuals and skills you are developing.

- Always be ready to serve as an advocate for those employees you coach and make sure they know what the opportunities are.

The most effective coaches seem to always know when the time is right and when it isn't to offer coaching to the team members they work with. They know that there are times when the circumstances are ideal to provide instructional support while there are others that aren't so appropriate.

Let's start by discussing those times when coaching should not be attempted...

- First of all you should <u>NEVER</u> attempt to coach an employee when you're angry, frustrated, or mad. Doing so will almost always lead to a negative experience for the employee. And, this is especially true if you're upset with the employee you intend to coach.

- It's also typically not a good idea to attempt a coaching session when things are hectic or especially busy in the office or shop. Coaching always works better when there's a little time for some unhurried discussion or practice.

- Be careful how you coach in front of customers or those not part of your organization. Unless absolutely necessary (for example if a key rule, policy, or process is being ignored) you should never insert yourself into a conversation between a member of your team and an outsider unless invited to do so.

The best times to coach are...

- When things are relatively quiet or a bit slower than usual are always good times to step aside to coach up individuals on the team.

- When you observe an employee using incorrect or improper techniques. And, unless the action is dangerous or improper in some significant manner, you should where possible wait until later when you can take the team member aside for a coaching discussion.

- It's <u>ALWAYS</u> a good time to coach individual employees when they ask for the opportunity. It might be a technique or process they need some help with. <u>NEVER</u> let these opportunities pass. Coaching is always more effective when the target employee is fully engaged and committed.

- Typically, it's best to schedule group coaching sessions at specific times unless an opportunity arrives where there's a lesson to be learned by the entire group.

If coaching is to be functional to the team in a manner that improves over-all productivity it must always be encouraging and uplifting, and when you attempt to do so at the wrong times or during the wrong circumstances it can defeat your purpose and actually become a barrier to the improvements you seek.

A coaches stopwatch...

1) Learn the best times to coach
2) Never coach when you are angry or mad
3) Don't attempt to coach when things are hectic and stressed
4) Keep it positive wherever possible
5) Never let a good opportunity to coach up pass you by
6) If they ask - just do it

There's a reason why so many top athletes fail miserably as coaches. They fail because most often they tend to be locked into their own perspective of what made them successful, so they in turn ask their players to be like them. And, as we know, there's a uniqueness to sports and athletic skills in particular that makes doing so by any coach a dysfunctional strategy. This is true also in the corporate world.

- It's a mistake to try to clone or copy ourselves regardless how successful our past might be.

- Every employee team member is unique and requires a different and unique approach.

- If we don't take care to be positive and encouraging in our coaching techniques we risk becoming the "harping complainer" that nobody pays attention to.

- If we don't choose the right times to coach it can get lost in the shuffle and lose its value.

- Coaching becomes time wasted if it isn't closely attached to measurable results and relevant job circumstances.

- If close attention isn't paid to best practices or established organizational methods the coach risks becoming an influence contrary to the desires and methodologies of the company to those he or she works with.

Over the years I've often said that coaching is a relatively simple business on the surface, but when you think about it coaching has some very complicated aspects in comparison to the classic instructor who typically has a well defined script and timeline to follow. A coach has none of these things in the majority of cases. Instead, a coach has to be ready to step in when circumstances warrant or opportunities appear. Most often he or she doesn't have a script to follow. Instead, he or she has to rely on his or her own experience and learned coaching skills.

And, just like during the ballgame, a good coach always knows how to stay out of the way when things are going just right and the team is playing to perfection. He or she also knows in the moment when to step in and offer positive support to make things better and more productive.

- He or she knows when to step in if it's important, for example if it's a safety or key procedural issue that can't wait until later.

- He or she also knows when not to step in if the situation isn't important enough to warrant him or her doing so.

At the end of the day there's a subtlety to the mentored coaching process that all of the good ones seem to instinctively understand and follow. They seem to always know just the right buttons to push with the right employee at just the right time. It's no coincidence at all that the best coaches in an organization are always the manager supervisors that everybody wants to work for and who always seem to have their talent bench full.

And guess what... these good and beloved coaching mentors were not born with their skills. They had to learn them at some point just like you.

Mentored coaching represents the classic "pay it forward" cultural mentality within an organization that can guarantee not only improved processes and results, but will also always make sure that the pipeline of talent and experience remains full.

How many times have you heard it said in an organization that there appears for some reason to be a dearth of talent coming up through the ranks? I've certainly heard it a lot over the years... and I have to tell you that those doing the asking need to honestly look themselves in the mirror to see who's to blame.

Yes, it's true that talent can be brought on board by going outside the organization to hire and bring it in. And, it should be done. However, just like the pro sports team who discovers that its reliance on "free agents" to stay competitive is difficult and expensive, a business who relies entirely on outside talent to remain successful takes a great risk that there will be huge gaps at some point in the employee "talent pool."

In addition to hiring the right people with the necessary skills you will need in the future, it's a well defined mentored coaching process within the organization that will guarantee that the talent pool and pipeline remains relevant to your future needs.

"Want a promotion, then train your replacement"

Ever hear this expression made? Or better yet, how about "I can't promote you because I have nobody to replace you with." And frankly, it's this situation more often as not that's the real conundrum for many organizations, because in many cases a desired growth is limited by a shortage of people talent.

This is part of the whole "talent pipeline" discussion we started earlier. For an organization to be in the position it needs and wants to be in so that it can harness the talent it has, it must keep a close eye on developing what I call "replacement talent." And, this is not only essential to the organization as a whole, it's also a key consideration to a manager who focuses on his or her coaching techniques in a way that positions his or her team members for future promotion.

This is important for the simple fact that all focused mentoring coaches have discovered... which is that when you coach well, your team members improve and do well, then as they do well they get recognized and promoted, which then leaves you in the position of having to replace them.

The Coaches Ultimate Objective

This leads us to the ultimate objective any true coach always has, which is to pay it forward for the training and mentoring he or she undoubtedly received from another by not only coaching up other team members, but also by putting them in position to be promoted. And this my friends is what truly makes an organization not only dynamic but keeps it sustainable with its talent pool for the long haul.

So, here's what well organized and focused mentoring coaches always do:

- They coach up all those they supervise to position them for future promotion.

- While coaching skills and processes for an employee's current position they are at the same time preparing him or her for that next position.

By doing so the managerial coach always insures that his or her "talent bench" is full with a replacement ready to step in when the time comes for a team member to be promoted or moved into another position in the organization.

The forward thinking and well organized mentoring coach does two things to keep his or her "talent bench" full:

- He or she is always coaching up the members of his or her team for the next position in their individual career paths.

- Knowing this is the case and that doing so ultimately leads to openings on his or her team, he or she is always on the lookout for prospective new team members. As such, he or she is always recruiting for when the time comes.

Want to do more than just read about Coach to Win?

Here's how. All you need to do is contact us at *TRAIN2WIN* to sign up for your own customized Coach to Win Program designed for the specific needs of your organization and employees.

- Need to coach up your sales force to increase their productivity and sales? We can help you do it with a coaching model that's based on our proven *TRAIN2WIN* techniques customized fully to your circumstances and methods.

- Maybe you need to get better results from your counter personnel who provide service to your customers. Not only can we help you set up a customer service process that's fully customized to your business, but we can also provide the coaching you need to teach your management personnel how to use it properly with their teams.

- How about those industry experts in your organization that you've targeted to conduct training sessions for their peers? We can help you with both our **Making Winning Presentations** publication (also available for purchase on Amazon.com) and our *TRAIN2WIN* **Coach To Win Program** to turn your subject experts into dynamic and effective presenter / instructors.

- Or, maybe you need to do some harassment training with your team and don't want to spend the high cost it takes to buy a program. We can help. You decide what you want to say to your employees, and we will coach up those you identify to make the presentations. Let me note that for those who are interested *TRAIN2WIN* does also offer it's complete **No Harassment Zone Training Program** and it's **No Harassment Zone Publication** (Amazon.com).

Here's how it all works:

- You select the subject matter for the coaching you want *TRAIN2WIN* to help you design (sales, customer service, etc...).

- We will work closely with you to design the kind of customized coaching processes that you are looking for so they work for your unique needs.

- As we work together to design the coaching materials, you will at the same time be identifying which employees you want to include in the training.

- Once all of the coaching materials have been created and the participants selected, we will then schedule 2 full coaching sessions with each of your identified employees.

- At the end of the 2nd coaching session, your employee will have the opportunity to do his or her own filmed presentation for analysis and review.

- Following the completion of the 2nd coaching session, your employee will receive a certificate of completion from *TRAIN2WIN,* and you will receive a full analysis of the sessions that include our recommendations.

The total cost for our *TRAIN2WIN* **Coach to Win Program** is designed to be both affordable and structured to your unique requirements.

- The client pays a one-time $500.00 development fee that helps us defray the cost of the materials we design and create. The fee is the same regardless how many employees you intend to have us coach.

- You will then pay a flat rate of $400.00 per participate that you identify and enter into the training. Let me be honest here and say that even we at *TRAIN2WIN* can't always guarantee just how well your employees will do with the coaching we offer. But, we do guarantee that we will do all that we say and will put every effort we have into making your people better. If you don't think we have done so, tell us and we'll try harder.

- When we've completed all of the coaching we've agreed to do with your employees to your satisfaction, all of the materials that we create together become yours to keep and use in the future as you wish. All that we ask is for the right to use them as examples for future clients.

We at *TRAIN2WIN* think you will agree that our **Coach to Win Program** is the most affordable and cost effective employee coaching program in the industry today.

T2W — TRAIN2WIN COACH TO WIN CHECKLIST

		YES	NO
(1)	You have an active coaching process in place	☐	☐
(2)	Your process includes training for coaches	☐	☐
(3)	Your process requires a commitment from employees	☐	☐
(4)	Your coaching is aligned to your goals & objectives	☐	☐
(5)	You have a monitoring system in place that allows you to make sure that you stay relevant and productive	☐	☐
(6)	You're receiving feedback and responding to the information you receive	☐	☐
(7)	Do you have a rewards / incentive program in place for your most effective mentor coaches?	☐	☐
(8)	Is your coaching process aligned to and does it support all of your career path needs and objectives?	☐	☐
(9)	Can you say that your mentored coaching is helping you keep your talent pool up to date and full?	☐	☐

There are no right answers to this self check, but it will hopefully give you an opportunity to work on the most important aspects of organized coaching in a winning way that both supports your objectives and provides the unique training experience your participants are looking for.

TRAIN2WIN* Publications** are authored by Thom Mindala, President and CEO of ***TRAIN2WIN LLC, and longtime training professional in the Paint and Coatings Industry. With a broad experience in employee based training initiatives and programs Thom brings a perspective to the consulting business that's both unique and dynamic.

Thom has a dedicated passion for all aspects of the training process, especially as they relate to the business and corporate worlds. He's convinced that the frustration that so many organizations experience when they undertake the training process with their members is not only solvable, but unnecessary.

If you have questions or comments about this or any other ***TRAIN2WIN*** Publication, you can direct them to Thom personally by using one of the following methods:

Telephone: 303-947-8989

Email: TMindala@gmail.com

Website: Train2win.weebly.com

If you would like to know more about Thom's training philosophy or about ***TRAIN2WIN LLC***, you can purchase a copy of the ***TRAIN2WIN* Manifesto** or the ***TRAIN2WIN* Presentation Guide** on Amazon.com. The Manifesto spells out in detail Thom's entire philosophy about training, and how it should and can work. The Presentation Guide details much of his philosophy while explaining the wide range of training opportunities that ***TRAIN2WIN LLC*** offers it's clients.